HOW TO EARN A

FORTURE

IN

THE CLEANING INDUSTRY

WITHOUT CLEANING A THING

June Morrison, Jr.

ISBN 978-0-615-25487-6

TABLE OF CONTENT

6.) FINDING THE CONTRACT AND CLOSING THE DEAL

1.)<u>INTRODUCTION</u>

CONGRATE, you are about to embark upon what could be

Consider one of the most exciting home based businesses

around today with unlimited potential. Allow me to share my

journey with you, and how I discovered this incredible

untapped market. A little over twenty years ago I was

employed with a multinational Janitorial corporation that

employed thousands of people. I started as a contract

worker working part time and soon moved into a full time

supervisory position. With my new title, I began to examine

the cleaning industry as whole, methods, marketing, profit

and lose. I would talk with those in management about any

and every thing related to the cleaning industry. The

company I worked for had cleaning contract all over the

country, and I wondered how small to medium size cleaning

company competed for contracts. What type of marketing

budgets were they working with and who within the

organization was responsible for securing bid leads

announcement or actually closing the deals. As my curiosity

grew, the need to have this and other questions addressed

became an obsession. I acquired the names and phone

numbers of cleaning services within a 50 mile radius of where I lived. As I called upon these cleaning professionals, many were open to share the inter working of their operations and areas they felt needed improvement. To my amazement almost all owners worked full time within their company, some were even involved in the day to day cleaning of office properties. Also, almost every owner worked during the evening or the night shift leaving little time to secure additional business. What was consistent from company to company was that many lack the skills necessary to submit a well thought out bid, and wish they had someone else within their operation that could handled

this responsibility. I realized that I had stumbled onto

something very special, a niche market that had the

potential of being very profitable for me and the clients that

I would represent. Now, I needed to know if what I was

proposing to do would be received by cleaning services of

all sizes. I ran an advertisement piece in the local

newspaper, detailing the nature of my service and how I

could help. By the end of the first week I had received an

unbelievable number of inquiring. They ask questions about

my service, the fees, my marketing approach and anything

that came to their mines, and so my journey began. You

mission if you choose to accept, will be to locate cleaning

contracts for the clients you will represent. Almost every

sector of the commercial cleaning industry competes for

cleaning contracts through a competitive bid process that is

normally open to all cleaning professional that meet

requirement established by the agency requesting such a

proposal. It is important that you screen your prospects

carefully; inadequate insurance or an inability to pay you

could mean disaster for your business. I recommended

charging a monthly retainer fee plus a commission for your

services, which I will discuss later in detail.

In close,
Have fun as you help others build their business, and they help grow your.

2.)<u>HOW TO LOCATE THE CLEANING SERVICES</u>

You may discover that obtaining cleaning service

professional as Clients may be one of your easier tasks you

encounter in building you Consultant practice. The fact is,

many cleaning services maybe more Than happy to have

you represent their company's interest in the Market place if

you can show them why teaming with your firm to Obtain

locate contracts can be mutually beneficial for their

company And yours. First, to get a feel for the industry and

the demand for you services, check your Sunday news

paper under the business Section, with the key word being

cleaning or janitor. Likewise do a webs search for cleaning

services in your area. Craig's list, Yahoo, Google, MSN, Ask

and others free or low cost adverting and Search engine

tools should provide you with several companies to choose

from. The cost of advertising is a factor for most small

Businesses, so these sites maybe a great place to start your

search for clients. Also, you want to place ads for the

services your company provide in some of these same

publications or on the free or low cost Web sites. I have

included several ads pieces at the end of this guide that

you may use in your marketing, which may be helpful as

you grow your practice? If at all possible, minimize your

search and ad placement to within about 50 Miles radium of

your home base. You will learn that many of you clients are

family people who, like you operate their businesses from

their home or a garage, van, or a car. These business

owners are looking to establish locate residential and

commercial contracts. Your goal is to write down or printout

the names and phone numbers of as many cleaning service

that you feels comfortable contact in your area. If the

owners name is included in the listing, write them down and

used them as your first point of contact. Before you make

your first call; make certain that you are in a quiet place

with limited distraction, projecting a professional image for

your firm should be of upmost importance. In Most instances

when you call, you will be speaking will with one of the

owners or the owner himself/herself. I was once contacted

by two partners regarding my services and agree To meet

at one the partner home while they were in the middle of a

Sunday football game, it does happen. Your objective at

this point is Just to set and appointment, not to get into the

entire meeting on the Phone. Many cleaning professional

work in their operation almost Primary at night, for them to set aside time during those precious day Light hours are quite rare, but if it means increasing their bottom line They will make the acceptation. Began calling from the list you compiled of cleaning professional in your area. Introducing yourself, as a cleaning consultant, inform the business owners that your company assists cleaning services in locating, bidding and securing commercial contracts, and that you would love to meet with him/her to discuss farther, how your firm may be able to help. Do not get into the cost of your service over the phone; we'll save that for the meeting. Remember as I pervious mentioned, these folks work in their operations and have little time to go after several contract at once. So meeting you may be music to their ears. You should always be moving in the direction of setting an appointment to meet with the client at their convenience. In the next section we'll discuss how you'll select the clients you want to represent and what to look for.

3.)CHOOSING THE RIGHT CLIENT

Whenever I meet a new client, I am actually interviewing

them to determine whether or not I want to work with them

and how we can both affect each other's lives. You already

use an effective screening tool, that little mental checklist

you automatically run when you meet a prospect. You get

that gut feeling about a person based on years of successes

with clients and even when you get burned. I have learned

over the years that one of the key components in forming a

Successful business relationship requires integrity. Integrity

can best be defined as the quality of possessing and a

steadfast adherence to high moral principles. All are

business qualities that you should look for in your prospects

and hopeful these are values found in you. Without integrity,

there little or no trust and the relationship will eventually fail.

Do you want happier clients? Then add integrity to your

customer service. You will find that not only will your clients

appreciate you more, but they will do more business with

your Consultant Practice and refer more clients to you.

Suggested Checklist

1. Understanding the prospects needs will help you to

discover whether you'll make or lose money servicing them.

2. Can the prospect afford your services? Ask for a list of

vendors that the prospect does business with. Inquire as to the

client's ability to meet fiduciary responsibilities.

3. Understand who has the final authority and will be signing

your checks.

4. Ask yourself if this business arrangement with this prospect

is a good fit.

5. Your clients should have from six months to one year of

operational and managerial cleaning experience.

6. Insurance is very important. If they don't have it, encourage them to get it as soon as possible. Larger contract require it, and usually detail those requirement in some type of summary page to perceptive bidder. Inadequate insurance may hurt your chance of bidding on some contracts.

7. Reliability is equally as important. Obtain references from your prospects, of contracts that they currently serve or cleaning services they have worked for. You'll discover that about 95% of all contract secured by you will want references on your clients.

4.)<u>YOU, YOUR CLIENT & YOUR FEE</u>

Sometimes business relationship get off to a great start, and

other times the bonding of a business relationship never

happens. Face it, people are people and communication

can break down for myriads of different reasons. As a

professional consultant you need the assurance, that for the

time and effort you put into locating contracts for your

clients you are paid on the basis of the terms of the

agreement. You will enter into an agreement with a client,

who you have not proven your abilities to, nor has the client

demonstrated an ability to pay as agreed. For this reason I

recommend entering into a 3 month agreement with your

clients. A monthly retainer may be necessary because

some proposals may take two or three months to close. This

can result in you spending many hours on the phone or

visiting the prospective locations several times. The 3-month

retainer is recommended because it assures your client that

if, in three months a contract has not been obtained, he/she

can discontinue any contractual arrangement that was

established between you and the client. I have included an

agreement that you can use and modify to fit your

particular need, but advocate that you seek professional

legal advice before entering into a contract. In addition to

the 3-month retainer, a percentage of the contract may be

included when forming the agreement. Let's use a rather

simple example to illustrate how you can structure payment

arrangement with your client. If this is you first project with

this client, and say the project has the potential of bringing

in $100,000 annually to your client. You might ask for $400-

600 per month retainer to cover expenses. Now should your

client win the bid and is issued a contract in the amount of

$100,000 over the terms of the agreement, you can establish

a 3-10% ongoing percentage of that amount every month

for the duration of the contract. And as you obtain

additional contracts a new agreement is entered into. There

is no limit to the number of cleaning contracts that you can

acquire, or the number of cleaning services you can serve

simultaneously. **Are you starting to get the big picture**

now!

5.)<u>TO BID OR NOT TO BID</u>

Most professional cleaning contracts are secured through

competitive bidding. With larger jobs, a well thought out bid

proposal is essential if consideration is even given. For

example, you may discover that a downtown 10 story

building was just built and management was accepting bids

for the job. Before you decide to look at the job, make

certain that you have the clients under contract that can

handle a particular project of this magnitude. Next, call the

building manager for information concerning cleaning

specification, square footage, etc. this will give you a feel

for what you may be up against. I have included a copy of

a cleaning specification at the end of the guide to show you

what is required by the customer even before a proposal is

submitted. Included also is a letter detailing square footage

of the properties involved. Upon arriving at the location,

conduct a thorough inspection of the building. If outlined

specification are given follow them as closely as possible,

being careful not to overlook any areas. If cleaning

specification is not provided, remember to bring a note pad

and make reference to every area outlined. A tape

measure might serve as a helpful tool if square footage isn't

readily available. I don't know of any person who has ever

submitted a bid on a particular job who didn't feel that their

bid was too high or too low. This area just takes practice.

You need to maintain a level of confidence and clear

thought when computing your bid. Remember that your

effort will reflect your client's performance on the job, i.e. if

the job you obtain was bid to low, it might result in low

productivity. Smaller jobs aren't as complicated and usually

a verbal arrangement can be made. To tell you that there is

one way of computing a bid would be far from the truth.

Nevertheless, each contract will differ from job to job.

Let's assume that you were bidding on a job that required
your client to:

<u>Clean Daily- Monday thru Friday</u>

Vacuum, high dust, remove trash, wipe desk

<u>Alternate- four time a year</u>

Clean windows inside and outside

<u>Suggested Approaches to Computing your Bid</u>

1. Determine cleaning time

2. Determine how many days in the month it will take to

clean the project.

3. Estimate cleaning time for alternate.

4. Compute the number of actual man hours that will be

worked in a given month.

5. Find out what your client is paying his workers per hour as labor and if a higher rate is paid out for alternate. Example of a formula that could be used:

Labor x estimated cleaning time plus maybe 10-15% for

indirect cost

The general consensus here is to come in with a bid you are

happy with and one that will make your client's profit

margin increase. Remember, you make money not only on

a retainer basis, but also on a percentage of each contract

secured. Do not limit yourself to only going after the larger

contracts. A lot of the smaller contract can be close rather

quickly and could show profit much faster.

6.)FINDING THE CONTRACT AND CLOSING THE DEAL

I am sure you have walked into a building or restaurant and

noticed that the floors were dirty or that the carpet had

stains. It's a fact that some cleaning services perform well

and others don't. Your search for contracts will not only

bring you to the doctor and the lawyers but also the CEO of

high rise properties. The need for competent professional

cleaning services cannot be overlooked. You local mega

plex theatre might be a good starting point, or the doctor,

dentist, or a friend of a friend might know of a real-estate property that is seeking cleaning service bids. As a cleaning consultant, it's your job to present a list of available clients that you have agreement with, to the prospective customer seeking cleaning services. In my experience, professionalism was one of the most important assets in the search for cleaning contracts. Building manager and other who accept invitation for bids tend to grade you on how well you handled yourself. So go with your "A" game. Upon talking to these individuals, inform them that you represent many cleaning services and that one of the services can handle whatever cleaning needs they may have. Listen to their needs, and ask for a general tour of the property. Ask if

any other cleaning service have submitted bids for the job.

Some will say and others will not. If at all possible, ask when

a decision will be made on your proposal. This will give you

an idea of how fast you will have to get your proposal in. If

there is no indication of when a decision is made, allow

about a week and call them back. When you call back if

your bid was declined, thank the customer and send out a

thank you card as a show of appreciation. You will find that

good business practices go a long way. Now should the

need for services arise again, they will remember you. But,

on the other hand if your bid is accepted set an

appointment at the customer's convenience. At this point

you should have matched a service with the requirement of

the proposal. Bring your client with you to the appointment

to meet the person(s) in charge. You should have your

client's contract ready for signing by the property manager

or whoever has been given the responsibility to handle such

matters. Most contracts between cleaning services and

property owner are usually for a period of 12 to 36 months

and can be renewed automatically unless there is a

problem. Now, after the contract is signed and all parties

involved are happy, your job is done. In about three months

call the property owner/manager to measure your client

progress. The decision to take on more clients at this point is

up to you, but knows your limits.

<u>Sample Contract</u>

This AGREEMENT between _____

Hereinafter referred to as _____

An independent Cleaning Services, hereinafter referred to

as _____

WHEREAS, cleaning service has agreed to furnish said

services for the monthly money consideration as set forth in

the bid form which is made a part of this contract.

NOWTHEREFORE, in consideration of the mutual promise and

covenants each to the other hereinafter made and set forth

in the monthly money consideration for the services

described and set forth in the attached bid form

specification, the parties here agree as follows:

1. The monthly charge for said maintenance service as

offered by cleaning service on the attached bid form and

accepted by _____

_____ shall be due and payable
on

The_____ of each month, provided that the work or

services required to be performed shall have been fully and

satisfactorily completed on the date.

2. It is mutually agreed and understood that this contract

shall become null and void upon 30 day written notice to

each party. In event of cancellation by either party,

payment for fractional month shall be determined by

prorating the monthly account on the basis of the number of

days involved.

4. The cleaning service has the required bonding insurance

and render

_____ Harmless
against any judgment or any expense in connection with
the work.

In WITHNESS WHEREOF, the parties have hereunder set their

hands and seal this _____ day of _____

, 20____

<u>Sample BID PROPOSAL</u>

Gentlemen:

After careful examination of the general

conditions of the site, the materials and labor

required, the undersigned proposes as follows:

To supply all labor, equipment and materials to
perform the contracted work:

For a monthly sum of _____
Annually_____

Alternate #1 Windows
washing_____Monthly_____

Alternate#2 Light fixture
washing_____Monthly_____

Sample request for bids

January

25, 2007

Dear Mr. Smith

Please be advised that we are now accepting bids

for the following property locations:

1. <u>Corporate Square</u>

a. 800 Bay West

B.800 Bay East

112,749 Square Feet

2. <u>Executive Square</u>

10001 West Lake

116,481 Square Feet

Enclosed you will find a sample copy of our cleaning

specifications. Note that these are only sample for

your review and will not become binding until a

contract is executed. The deadline for submitting bids

will be March 1, 2007.

Steve Beach

Property Manager

Sample copy of cleaning specification

Corporate Professional Building

A. <u>Daily</u>

Empty trash receptacles sweep entrances, lobbies and

corridors. Damp mop and buff all floors in mail corridors,

sweep and/or vacuum traffic patterned areas in the office

and extend sweep or vacuum to remove obvious dirt from

around and under the furniture. In office areas, dust all

horizontal surface that are readily available and visibly

require dusting. Spot carpet to remove stains.

B. Every Other day

Sweep and vacuum stair landing and steps. Police garage

areas.

C. Weekly

Sweep sidewalk, parking areas and driveways.

D. Every two weeks

Damp mop and spray buff all floors in secondary entrances,

lobbies and corridors and all office areas.

E. <u>Monthly</u>

Thoroughly dust all horizontal surface or furniture in office

area. Thoroughly vacuum and spot clean carpet and/or

sweep full floor areas in office space.

<u>Executive Square</u>

Cleaning Specification:

<u>Offices, Conference Rooms, Lunch and Vending</u>

Empty Wastebasket

Dust or damp wipe furniture

Dust mop, sweep or vacuum floor

Spot clean walls, columns, carpet and floors

Dust windows sills and perimeter heaters

Wipe spills or smears from vending machine

Wash waste cans in vending area, if needed

Lavatories

Fill all paper towel, napkin and soap dispensers

Wash mirrors, basins commodes and urinals

Damp wipe shelves, partitions and ledges

Spot clean doors and walls

Polish chrome and stainless steel fixtures and plumbing

Empty all waste receptacles

Sweep and mop floors

Miscellaneous

Clean all entrance door glass

Clean all glass in interior door

Close all windows

Wash and polish drinking fountains

Fill paper cup dispensers

Clean all chalkboard unless told otherwise

Sweep porch, sidewalk

Remove trash from building

Police and sweep the evaluation area

Dust all items hanging from walls once each week

Be thoroughly familiar with emergency call list and pertinent

procedures.

Contractor's Responsibility for damage- Any damage

caused by the Contractor shall be repaired at the

Contractor's expense. The Contractor shall save and keep

harmless the Owner and Owner's employees from any and

all claims for damage to persons or property sustained

during the prosecution of the work.

Insurance required- The Contractor will furnish the Owner

with originals or photo copies of their continuous blanket

policies for the following:

A.)Worker's Compensation insurance as required by the law

B.) Bodily Injury Liability insurance with limits of not less than

$500,000 for each person and $500,000 for each accident.

C.) Property Damage Liability insurance shall be filed with

the Owner and shall be subject to the Owner's approval.

<u>Sample Ad Copies</u>

"Looking for Cleaning Contracts we can

help"

Call your Company name and phone number

Just started a Cleaning business or

thinking about starting one, Let us

locate your bids and secure your next

contract.

Call your Company name and phone number

Growing your Cleaning Service is as

easy as calling, your Company name and phone

number! We'll show you our proven method of success.

"Your Cleaning business could be

earning over $100,000 this year call" your

Company name and phone number

We can help you build your cleaning

service 1 contract @ a time! Your Company

name and phone

www.ingramcontent.com/pod-product-compliance
Lightning Source LLC
Chambersburg PA
CBHW021916190326
41519CB00008B/803